This publication is designed to provide accurate and
authoritative information in regard to the subject matter
covered. It is sold with the understanding that neither the
author nor the publisher is engaged in rendering legal,
investment, accounting, or other professional services.
While the publisher and author have used their best
efforts in preparing this book, they make no
representations or warranties with respect to the
accuracy or completeness of the contents of this book
and specifically disclaim any implied warranties of
merchantability or fitness for a particular purpose. No
warranty may be created or extended by sales
representatives or written sales materials. The advice and
strategies contained herein may not be suitable for your
situation. You should consult with a professional when
appropriate. Neither the publisher nor the author shall
be liable for any loss of profit or any other commercial
damages, including but not limited to special, incidental,
consequential, personal, or other damages.

Author's Note

I would like to thank my daughter for her encouragement to publish my thoughts on interview preparation and execution. Her contributions to the content and input with the editing were priceless and greatly appreciated!

Before you are a leader, success
is all about growing yourself.
When you become a leader,
success is all about growing
others.

-Jack Welch

Taking the First Step

Peter M. Leahy

Introduction

My name is Peter Leahy. I spent more than 40 years in the sales and marketing space, working mostly for large consumer packaged goods companies. I had the opportunity to learn and grow as I worked for great companies like Johnson and Johnson®, PepsiCo® (Frito-Lay®), Coca Cola®, and the Coors Brewing Company®. I also worked with some smaller privately held or start-ups and family-owned companies and owned my own franchise business for 5 years. During the course of my career, I interviewed many times, including for internal promotions or with new companies when I was looking to expand my career. I also interviewed countless numbers of candidates to work with me and for me along the way.

Through first-hand experience, I learned many things that helped me perform better in interviews. Likewise, when I was looking to fill positions, I also observed and learned from the differences among candidates. I was amazed by how unprepared many candidates were when they arrived in my office. It is from all my experience on both sides of the interview table, as a candidate and a hiring manager, that I have created this step-by-step process to help you prepare to conduct great interviews. It is important to note that there are two parts to a job search: interview acquisition and interview execution. While interview acquisition is important and there are lessons to learn that can significantly improve your ability to obtain interviews, this book will focus on the latter. This book was written with interview execution in mind and will benefit those who are in the job search flow and want to sharpen their interviewing skills.

As you read this book, keep in mind that every interview is different! Every manager may have their own style of interviewing. Every company may have different or unique processes. It is impossible to guess how the interview process will go. The key is to control what you can control: your preparation and performance. The more prepared you are, the more confident you will be that you can handle anything a company might present you. At the end of each chapter, I have included a short story about real life experiences with interviews—good and bad—so make sure to check them out. Let's dive into the process!

Overview

*A journey of a thousand miles begins with a single
step*
— Confucius

One of the most important lessons I've learned throughout my career is that getting a job **is a job** in and of itself. You must dedicate time to prepare yourself for the process. By **taking the first step**, I am asking you to **COMMIT** to the process of getting a job. That means that you are committing to the process of preparing and practicing until you can execute your answers flawlessly. The great news is that the preparation is cumulative and once complete, you can use your work repeatedly throughout your career. My method for interview preparation will work for anyone, at any stage of their career, from entry level to senior executive. The process is straightforward and if you do the work in advance, you will arrive at your interviews (in my opinion) more prepared and confident than 95 percent of candidates.

The purpose of this book

One of my favorite questions to ask the people I mentor about interviewing is "what is the purpose of a job interview?" It is interesting to me how many people respond that the purpose of a job interview is to get a job! While that may sound logical, the answer shows that most people do not fully understand the process.

What I didn't fully grasp until I had spent time hiring is that for 99 percent of job interviews, the assured result very likely will be another interview. Very few people walk into a business on their first interview and land a job offer. So, in actuality **the purpose of a job interview is to get another interview**...and ultimately those inter-views should lead to a job offer!

Interviewing is a process not an event. It takes time in preparation and practice for flawless execution to go from candidate to new hire. It is critical for the job seeker to completely understand this premise, as it is the basis on which the following training will be built.

Throughout the book, I will walk through each step in this process so that anyone reading along will be able to prepare themselves, effectively organize their thoughts and documents, and execute an interview in a professional manner and say the right things to generate callbacks.

Ultimately, the purpose for this book is to help YOU, the candidate, get a better understanding of the interview process from start to finish and to build a toolbox of skills, techniques, and processes that will allow you to generate:

CONFIDENCE: solid preparation will build more confidence

UNDERSTANDING: a better understanding of how the process works and what the companies are looking for

EXECUTION: executing interviews at a high professional level that will move you to the top of the list of candidates

Each one of these modules should prepare you to take the next step and I encourage you to work through each one as it relates to your ongoing job search or interview process!

Table of contents

Chapter 1

Discovery: What am I good at?

Be yourself; everyone else is already taken.
— Oscar Wilde

When a company decides to hire someone, it is because they have a specific need. There is a role that is necessary to make the company successful and they need to find the right person to fill that role. The hiring manager working with the Human Resources (HR) department develops a job description. It details the hard and soft skills a candidate must have to be considered for the role. Once this is finalized, the HR department will generally post the job both internally and externally.

While the job description will be very detailed, the bottom line is that the hiring manager wants to know three things about each candidate. Companies use the interview process to answer these three questions, and as a candidate, these

1

questions are critical to understand as you navigate the interview process.

1. Can they do the job?
2. Will they do the job?
3. Will they fit into our culture?

Preparing your responses to these questions requires some introspection: the more you know yourself, the better prepared you'll be to respond. One suggestion I have is that you spend some time getting to know yourself. A great way to start is to take a Meyers Briggs test or another personality profile test.[1]

Preparation for the interview process starts with developing a comprehensive understanding of your skills and attributes, or "soft skills." Soft skills are generally skills that stem from your personality, although they can be developed over time with practice (like interviewing!). "People skills" is usually the term most associated with soft skills. These skills are generally harder to quantify and are best explained using real world

---

[1] Some other examples include **DiSC** (https://www.mydiscprofile.com/en-us/free-personality-test.php); **Strengths Finder 2.0:** by Douglas Clifton (Available on Amazon); **Personality testing:** (https://www.16personalities.com/free-personality-test)

stories that you can use to show the interviewer how you used or exhibited a skill.

Hard skills are skills that you can learn or for which there are tangible "market signals" that you have a demonstrated proficiency. These skills include things like a degree in French, a certification in your industry, or proficiency with Microsoft Office® (Word®, Excel®, PowerPoint® etc.). We will discuss "Hard Skills" in a moment. In this exercise we will focus only on soft skills.

One of the most challenging aspects of job interviews for most people is talking about themselves in a positive manner. Not everyone struggles with this, but a lot of people do. If you find this to be a challenge, I am confident that you will find what follows to be extremely helpful.

Examine the list of attributes found in the following chart (**Figure 1**). Take a few minutes and circle every attribute on the list that you feel is a strength. Don't agonize over your choices—use your instinct: if you think you demonstrate the skill most or some of the time, go ahead and circle it. If there's an attribute not listed that you feel strongly about, please list that as well. We will refine your choices as we move through the exercise.

Figure 1: Attributes

☐ Administration	☐ Values	☐ Responsible
☐ Attendance	☐ Cooperative	☐ Independence
☐ Problem Solving	☐ Analytical	☐ Decision-making
☐ Judgment	☐ Productivity	☐ Appearance
☐ Delegation	☐ Presentations	☐ Coachability
☐ Fairness	☐ Negotiating	☐ Social Media
☐ Compassion	☐ Knowledge	☐ Dependability
☐ Leadership	☐ Professionalism	☐ Coaching (others)
☐ Flexibility	☐ Networking	☐ Strategic
☐ Honesty	☐ Performance	☐ Competent
☐ Patience	☐ Approachability	☐ Versatility
☐ Winner	☐ Personable	☐ Humor
☐ Concentration	☐ Integrity	☐ Perseverance
☐ Action-oriented	☐ Conscientious	☐ Initiative
☐ Persuasiveness	☐ Adaptability	☐ Creativity
☐ Innovative	☐ Planning	☐ Confident
☐ Follow-up	☐ Organization	☐ Self-motivated
☐ Wisdom	☐ Directing	☐ Learning Ability
	Others	
☐ Public Speaking	☐ Accuracy	☐ Drive
☐ Listening	☐	☐ Team Building
	Resourcefulness	
☐ Discretion	☐ Loyalty	☐ Achievement
☐ Conflict Resolution	☐ Goal Setting	☐ Openness
☐ Team Player	☐ Competent	☐ Budgeting
☐ Empathy	☐ Management	☐ Responsiveness
☐ Career Ambition	☐ Enthusiasm	☐ Caring
☐ Ethics	☐ Motivation	☐ Service
☐ Communication	☐ Gracious	☐ Operations
☐ Thorough	☐ Composure	☐ Hard Working
☐ Maturity	☐ People Person	☐ Articulate

I suggest you also make a few copies of this list and give them to two people who know you (friends, parents, etc.) and are willing to give you honest feedback. Once you have completed your list and your friends have given you theirs, compare them and look for consistencies. My guess is there will be at least 20 attributes that show up on everybody's list.

Next, get some 3x5 cards and write each of those twenty attributes on a separate card. Once your cards are completed, put them all in a stack and go through them one by one. Your goal is to start to focus on your top five strengths. As you go through the cards and you feel strongly about that skill, place the card off to the right. If it's not as strong, place it to the left. After this process, you should have about ten cards remaining in the left pile of strengths and ten cards that you placed to the right. Now, put the cards on the right (strengths) in order from one to ten with one being your strongest skill. Write these attributes down in that order with your strongest skill being first.

These ten attributes will form the basis of the next step of the process, which is to define in your own words why this skill or attribute is a strength. Your list might look something like this:

LEADERSHIP, INTEGRITY, TEAM PLAYER, WORK ETHIC, SELF MOTIVATED, DECISION MAKING, COACHABILITY, COMMUNICATION, ENTHUSIASM, FLEXIBILITY

Once you have completed this you will already be significantly more prepared than many of the other candidates that you will be competing with for your next job.

Here is an interesting reference point. These are the traits that the US Army looks for in Officer Candidates:

U.S. Army Traits of Character		
Bearing	Confidence	Endurance
Courage	Integrity	Tact
Decisiveness	Justice	Maturity
Initiative	Coolness	Improvement
Will	Assertiveness	Candor
Sense of humor	Competence	Commitment
Creativity	Self-discipline	Humility
Flexibility	Empathy	Compassion

Returning to the three questions, it's important to grasp that the third and final question, "Will they fit into our culture," ultimately has everything to do with the company itself. This is not to be confused with questions on diversity and inclusion but is simply a matter of business and skills. For example, a person who is very introverted or painfully shy may have a very difficult time being successful on a team that is primarily responsible for briefing clients or making live presentations. As an applicant, you may not always have a full picture of what is required in the day-to-day execution of the job, so this might be something you can find more out about during the interview process by asking questions.

Before we finish the chapter, I wanted briefly to touch on hard skills. While you need to make sure you have the key hard skills that a job requires, the hiring manager should be able to find most of these skills in your resume. These are typically verifiable facts, so it's important to not exaggerate. It may be appropriate to reference hard skills when telling a story during interview (we'll focus more on story telling in **Chapter 2**). Some job seekers I've mentored have expressed that referencing parts of their resume during the interview process makes them uncomfortable because they feel boastful or egotistical, but keep in mind that a prospective employer may only skim your resume, so a light reference back to a hard skill may help to reinforce that you are a fit for the job.

Interview story #1

A candidate was driving to an interview that was supposed to start at 9:00 am. He hit heavy traffic along the way and realized that he had not given himself enough time. He became very stressed and started driving very aggressively, weaving in and out of the traffic to make up time. As he turned into the parking garage, there was a man in front of him driving quite slowly and having a difficult time getting the parking gate to go up. The candidate was so frustrated he honked his horn and made some not so friendly gestures to the man in front of him. He finally parked, ran to the elevator, and arrived at the interview. When the hiring manager came out to greet him, it was the man in the car at the parking garage. Needless to say, the candidate 's interview didn't go well.

Moral of the story: Know exactly where you are going for an interview. Map it out and make sure you allow time for unexpected problems. Go a day early and get the route nailed down in advance. Being early always trumps being rushed!

Chapter 2

Developing Your Stories

There's always room for a story that can transport people to another place.
– J.K. Rowling

Congratulations on identifying the top 5-to-10 skills where you excel! This knowledge will form the foundation of confidence that we will build to get you mentally prepared for the interview. The next step of the process will be to bring these skills to life.

We will accomplish this by having you reach back into your life or work experiences to provide specific examples of how you identified and performed the specific skills that you have highlighted. For those already in the business world, it may be easier to identify work-related stories. For those looking to enter the workforce for the first time, don't shy away from supplementing work stories with life experiences.

It is important to note that I mentioned life experiences and business experiences. I have found that having life experience stories AND business stories provide companies with a more complete understanding of how you conduct yourself. It is acceptable to use a story from school, or even a personal event, to provide examples of your skills.

For example, I was helping a good friend of mine's daughter prepare for her first interview after graduating from college. She had been an athlete in college and had even served as the captain of her team during her senior year. Just imagine all the skills that she had to learn and exhibit to be an effective captain. The amazing thing was that she did not realize that it was okay to use these stories during an interview. I asked her to tell me a little bit more about her experience, and her stories demonstrated **leadership, discipline, organizational skills, motivation, planning, and follow-up**—all critical skills in athletics AND business. It just had never dawned on her that these skills were **"transferable"** to the workplace. I am here to tell you emphatically that they are.

We developed stories about her time as captain that related to each of the attributes highlighted above. Although she lacked work experience, it gave her increased confidence to know that she had hard-hitting examples of her skills to show to the companies she planned to meet with.

Let's look a little closer at the process of developing a good story for an interview.

The first thing to remember is that most interviews have a specific amount of time allocated to you by the interviewer. Usually, it can be anywhere from 15 to 60 minutes. That may sound like a lot of time, but it is not. For this reason, we must limit our stories to 60 to 90 seconds. Keeping our stories pithy and focused is critical. I recommend a popular storytelling methodology called **S.T.A.R.** to keep the storytelling on track (and avoid rambling).

This acronym stands for:

SITUATION

TASK

ACTION

RESULTS

You can use this as a formula to develop your stories relating to the skill that you would like to illustrate. Your challenge will be to dig back into your past and identify times that you encountered a situation that caused you to identify a task and take action to fix or complete the task. By taking this action, a specific result (or results) was generated. I will now walk through S.T.A.R. using an example so that we clearly understand the goal of each component. If you'd like, choose one of your own skills and follow along!

Interview question: *"Tell me about one of your strengths."*
Response: *"One of my core strengths is **problem solving.**"*

Situation: This portion of your story sets the scene. It provides the listener with an understanding of the context and environment in which you are working. Give the listener just enough background information to understand the situation that you were in. For my example, it might sound like this:

"I was working as a project manager for a large construction company. My boss was out sick, and a client called with a significant problem with our construction timeline. I did not have a clear responsibility to solve the problem, but with my boss out and the client demanding an answer, I had to think fast."

Task: The second phase of the story telling process is to identify the **task** or challenge you faced and

to lay out the problem clearly for the listener. It could sound something like this:

"Since there was no one in the department, I had to find a way to improve our construction timeline by at least 1 week to placate the customers' needs and make them happy."

Action: In this phase of the process, you tell the listener the specific things that you did to solve the problem. It could sound like this:

"I quickly reviewed the project and remembered that the legal team, responsible for all permitting, had asked to pad the timeline by 4 weeks due to a backlog at city hall for acquiring permits. I knew that, realistically, if they pushed a little harder, they could get the permits in 2 weeks and enable the next phase of construction to start sooner. After identifying this opportunity, I went to the legal department and explained the situation and the need to improve the timeline by a week. I asked for, and gained, their commitment to get the permits completed by the following week, eliminating 2 weeks from the timeline. I presented the problem and proposed solution to my boss' boss, the VP of Operations. She thought it was excellent and allowed me to notify the customer."

Result: This is the best part of the story, specifically what you were able to accomplish. In this case, the story ended this way:

"I left the VP's office and called the client. I walked them through our solution to gain a week on the project and they were very happy. The unexpected result was that at our next company meeting, I was singled out by the VP of Operations for my problem solving and commitment to customer service and given the Employee of the Month Award!"

Developing a concise story that provides a clear and tangible picture of the skills you possess is powerful! With each story you tell that clearly exemplifies the attributes you possess, your stock will go up in the eyes of the interviewer.

The key is to write out each story, just as I have here. You need to do this for each of your top five attributes. Once you have written them out, you need to memorize them word for word. And once you have memorized them you must practice telling them to friends and family members so that you get good at telling them in a concise and personal manner. A trick I like to use is to call a friend's (or your own) phone and leave the story as a message. See if you can tell the whole story before the time runs out!

Interview story #2

I was a young salesman and I had decided to look for a better opportunity. I had a number of interviews with a company and the hiring manager loved me. He told me over the phone that all was great, and he was scheduling me for a start date in 3 weeks, allowing me to give my 2 weeks' notice. I immediately told my boss, and to my shock and surprise, he terminated me on the spot. The following Monday, I received a call from the hiring manager of the new company. He informed me that the company had implemented an emergency hiring freeze and I would not be able to start until the freeze was lifted. Since I didn't have any confirmation of the offer other than his phone call, I was toast! He never called me back again.

Moral of the story: You do not have a job offer until you receive a detailed written confirmation of the offer in writing. We will talk more about this in Chapter 10.

Chapter 3

Understanding the Interview Process

*Nothing in life is to be feared, it is only to be understood.
Now is the time to understand more, so that we may fear
less.*
– Marie Curie

For discussion purposes, let's assume that you have created an impactful resume and started applying for jobs. The game really starts when you get that first call back. They want to talk to you! "YES," you say to yourself. So now the process begins.

Let's take a step back and examine the process from the employer's point of view. Something has happened to cause them to conduct a search to fill a position. Usually, one of four things sets this in motion: the incumbent was promoted, leaving a vacancy; a new position was created; a person resigned, causing the position to be open; or, a person was terminated, resulting in an opening.

The hiring manager calls the Human Resources department and asks them to start a search. The staffing person posts the job and job description on any number of job boards, and you find it and apply. Easy, right? Maybe for you, but not for the staffing person. In a tough job market, the company may receive hundreds, if not thousands, of applications. Many job postings have screening questions built into the online application system. Those questions are designed to filter out the candidates that do not meet the minimum requirements. You would be amazed, for example, by how many people apply for a job that requires both fluent English and Spanish but cannot speak both languages. Someone must filter these candidates out.

In today's world, many large companies employ technology and artificial intelligence (AI) to screen applicants. While that's not the focus of this book, the relevant implication is that when a job search is initiated, from the company's perspective the initial processes are all about eliminating candidates, rather than finding them. This is important to understand.

Imagine a search has been started and 500 resumes have been collected. Resumes are scanned for key words, skills attributes, and experience. Many are eliminated on the spot—

usually by staffing or hiring specialists rather than the "end user" office. The list is now down to roughly 100. The hypothetical next step would be a phone interview. Phone interviews are usually 15 to 30 minutes. Why? Because the HR professional has 100 people to call. The group of candidates is generally qualified, but now the list must be reduced to only the best candidates. The phone interview is about screening candidates and eliminating more resumes.

From the candidate's perspective, the goal in this scenario is to make the cut and move to the next step in the process. Remember that your goal in the interview is to get another interview, so everything you do should be focused on that. **REMEMBER THIS:** You rarely will get a job offer from a phone interview, but you can certainly lose the opportunity if you do not take the process very seriously. We will go into this, and additional steps to prepare for a phone interview in more detail in **Chapter 8**.

Once you have made the cut, you might be asked to participate in a second round of interviews. This process could follow one of several formats. There might be face-to-face interviews with HR team members, or a group or panel interview. Each company is going to be different. Depending on the position, this process may take weeks. The goal for the company is to continue to eliminate candidates until only one remains. Your job is to keep fighting until you are the one, they select! **The better you prepare the easier these become.**

Interview types and formats you might encounter:

Phone interviews
Zoom interviews
Fact-to-Face interviews
Team interviews (multiple interviewees)
Panel interviews (multiple interviewers)
Peer interviews
Personality or IQ profile testing
"Rubber Stamp" interviews

Interview Questions

Acknowledging this dynamic between the hiring officials (trying to narrow the pool of candidates) and the applicant (trying to get the job) is a mental game changer for your interview preparation. While a few people out there are naturally charismatic, I cannot tell you how many people I have spoken to over the years who simply hate the interview process and say that they are bad at "selling" themselves. Move past this mentality. When you see the hiring process as mechanical, it's easier to avoid letting your self-worth get wrapped up into the outcome, and I promise you that you'll perform better. Stay focused on the actions you need to take to be prepared at every step of the process.

Interview story #3

When my daughter was in graduate school, she desperately wanted to work with a specific professor as a teaching assistant. Not only would the position save her tens of thousands of dollars of debt, but it was a professor she really looked up to. She poured everything she had into this professor's class and did as much research as she could about the position, including speaking to every former teaching assistant she could find. When it came time for the interview, she unexpectedly was asked what she thought of one of her fellow students in the class. Without thinking about it, she responded that she felt the other student was more qualified for the position. Later, when asked if she had any questions, she said she had none (because in her mind she had already done the research). She got the job, but the professor later told her that she had made two nearly unforgivable mistakes—planting a seed that there was someone better out there for the position and seeming disinterested by not asking any questions.

Moral of the story: Sometimes there's a lot at stake during an interview, but if you let it, it will eat you alive. NEVER denigrate yourself, period, even if you are asked to speak to a skill that you think needs more development. If you are able to step back and focus on the process, rather than the outcome, you'll perform much better!

Chapter 4

Getting Prepared

"By failing to prepare you are preparing to fail"
– Benjamin Franklin

Great interviews are the result of great preparation. Great preparation starts with an organized approach to research. In this chapter I present the approach that has worked for me, which, all in all, should cost no more than about $15.

To organize everything, I will need for an interview, I start with a simple white three-ring notebook. The kind you can get at any office supply store for under $5. Make sure it has a clear plastic cover that allows you to slip a cover page in the front. This is especially important, but I will explain more later.

Also purchase a packet of tab dividers (10 tabs for $10). I am a fan of Avery® products, and they make a great set of tabs that include a printable

Table of Contents to really get you organized. Generic options are usually available, too.

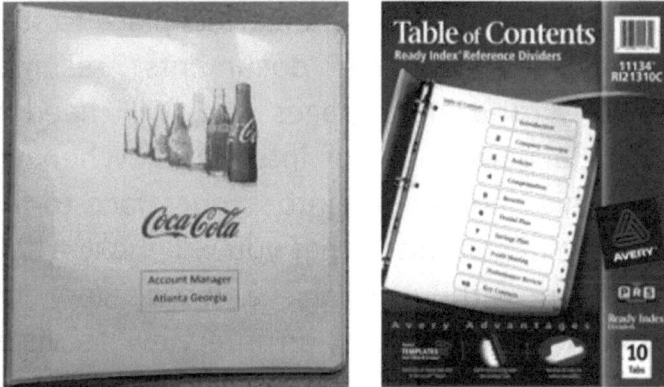

Now that you have your notebook and tabs, let's build this thing out! First, create a cover page. For this example, I am going to assume that I am interviewing for the position of Account Manager with one of my former companies, Coca-Cola. I would start by going to Google® Images and finding a nice image for Coca Cola. There are many images related to the company you are looking for, so just choose one that you like. You can copy and paste the image onto a blank word document. If you are in a hurry, you can always type the company name out, but if you are planning to bring the binder to the interview (which you should!), then the image demonstrates your attention to detail and willingness to go the extra mile. Also add the position for which you are interviewing on the front page.

This binder will serve as the perfect place to store all your job research documents, resumes, questions, and note pages you will need to execute a perfect set of interviews. When you carry this notebook into your face-to-face interviews, I guarantee that you will make a solid impression without saying a word. Very few candidates will arrive at an interview as visibly prepared as you. You want the interviewer to see your notebook. It is great if they ask you about it, too. You can, and should be, immensely proud of your preparation and it will make a subtle but powerful impression. Trust me!

The added value of creating this interview notebook is that it will be beneficial not only throughout the interview process for a multi-step process, but also as a template for other job interviews you might have—not much of the content will change. Some job interview processes, particularly for federal or government jobs, may span a period of several months, so the notebook will serve as a resource to refresh your memory on what you might have already learned. Similarly, the sections for questions, notes, and resumes will be needed for every interview and are easily transferrable. If you interview with a different company, change the cover page, and add tailored research for the new company in the appropriate tabs, saving the old research in case you need it again some point in the future.

You may wish to create an archive or master binder where you save all your previous research and resumes. It's amazing, over the course of your career, to see how you grow and the things that you learn! Everything related to your job search will build off the preparation you put in.

Interview story #4

*Another mistake I made when I was a young job seeker centered around a lunch interview. Interviews during a meal are tricky and full of pitfalls. I had flown on a 6:00 am flight to Chicago. I had to take the train downtown then I had to take a taxi to the hotel where I was going to lunch with the VP of sales of the company I was interviewing with. The hiring manager told me it was a slam dunk, and that the VP was excited just to meet me. I call this kind of interview a **"rubber stamp"** interview, more of a "meet and greet" session. As I found out, these kinds of interviews can be very dangerous. This was back when everyone wore a suit and tie to work every day. We were meeting at a very fancy hotel. By the time we sat down for* *lunch I was famished and ready to eat. The VP had brought a couple of his team members, and they all ordered hamburgers. That sounded delicious, so I had one too. When my burger arrived, I reached out and grabbed the burger with two hands and took a massive bite. It was so good! It was then that I noticed how quiet it was around the table. I looked up and saw the three company representatives staring at me in disbelief as they started cutting their burgers with a knife and fork and eating them piece by piece. They looked at me like I was a heathen. I never got a call back from the company, let alone the offer I expected!*

Moral of the story: If you have an interview that involves a meal, order a salad, and then don't eat it, push it around on your plate. You are not there to eat; you are there to impress the interviewer! Pay attention and eat something before or after the interview. It is a lot safer. Don't lose a potential job offer over a burger!

Chapter 5

Getting Organized

It takes as much energy to wish as it does to plan.
— Eleanor Roosevelt

Now that you have your notebook and blank tabs, let's talk about the kinds of things you will need to look for as you research the company that will be conducting your interview. You have room for 10 tabs and a few of them will be used for things you will need to carry with you to the interview. Remember, this is your notebook, so feel free to add or delete any tabs as you see fit. Here are some possible tabs:

1. Job Description
2. Company overview
3. Company Mission Statement
4. Company Vision and Values
5. Products and/or Services
6. Organizational structure
7. S.T.A.R. Stories
8. Questions
9. Note Pages
10. Resumes

Again, you can choose any tabs that work best for you. Below are some detailed thoughts on the utility of each tab that I selected and why they are important for my interview preparation process.

Job Descriptions

If possible, always retain a copy of the job description for the position you are applying for. Job descriptions provide great insight into what the hiring manager is looking for in the perfect candidate. They provide soft and hard skill requirements, as well as a list of responsibilities. Don't let a job description intimidate you. If you feel you have most of the skills and can handle the responsibilities, go for it. Everyone is always looking for the perfect candidate. NO ONE ever finds one. They choose the candidate who is the best fit.

Company Overview

This tab is where you place copies of any information you can find about the company. If the company is large enough, any financial website like Yahoo Finance can provide this type of information. The easiest is the company website.

Using Coca-Cola as an example, I went to their corporate page coca-colacompany.com. There, I was able to find a great deal of information about many things. The "Our Company" tab, for example, contains interesting statements reflecting company values that you would want to take note of in your research documents. For example:

> *We do business the right way,*
> *not just the easy way.*
> *People matter. Our planet matters.*
> *EXPLORE RESPONSIBLE BUSINESS*

The last line included a link to their page on sustainability. It provides you with tremendous insight into the company's beliefs, values, and commitments. Knowing this before you go into an interview can be helpful. The first tab alone on Coca-Cola's website has enough information to keep you reading for a while. While that is important, you need to keep digging. The next tab on their web site is Purpose and Vision.[2]

---

[2] https://www.coca-colacompany.com/

OUR PURPOSE:

Refresh the world. Make a difference

OUR VISION:

Our vision is to craft the brands and choice of drinks that people love, to refresh them in body & spirit. And done in ways that create a more sustainable business and better shared future that makes a difference in people's lives, communities, and our planet.

If you scroll down, you will see the heading:

WHO WE ARE:

Learn about our company's purpose and vision.

If you click on "**Read More**," it takes you to a nice clean chart that captures everything on one page. This should be saved in your interview notebook.

It looks like this:

WHO WE ARE
THE COCA-COLA COMPANY

PURPOSE
TO REFRESH THE WORLD.
MAKE A DIFFERENCE.

VISION
LOVED BRANDS, DONE SUSTAINABLY,
FOR A BETTER SHARED FUTURE.
Our vision is to craft the brands and choice
of drinks that people love, to refresh them in
body and spirit. And done in ways that create
a more sustainable business and better shared
future that makes a difference in people's lives,
communities and our planet.

HOW WE DO IT

LOVED BRANDS
- Passion for people and their lives
- Cutting-edge excellence in ingredients, innovation, design and marketing
- Investment for leadership across categories in purposeful brands that consumers love
- Act globally and locally
- Powerful partnerships with our bottling system to bring brands to life in the market

DONE SUSTAINABLY
- Start with facts, based in science
- Grow our business while reducing our sugar
- Make packaging a circular economy, with a focus on getting 100% collection to enable reuse for World Without Waste
- Be water balanced, improving water security where needed most
- Reduce our carbon footprint
- Source more sustainably and ethically

FOR A BETTER SHARED FUTURE
- Invest in employees' personal growth and talent
- Empower people's access to equal opportunities, build inclusion
- Create value for customers—big and the many small
- Support our local communities, both to achieve more and in times of need
- Deliver returns to our investors

BEHAVIORS WE FOCUS ON

WE NURTURE A CULTURE WITH A PASSION TO REFRESH THE WORLD. WE MAKE A DIFFERENCE.
We act with a growth mindset, take an expansive approach to what's possible, and believe in continuous learning to improve our business and ourselves. We value how we work as much as what we achieve. The behaviors we focus on every day are being:

CURIOUS
- Always seek, never settle
- Ask why or why not, or what if, or I wonder

EMPOWERED
- Own it, take accountability
- Each one of us can make a big difference

INCLUSIVE
- Leverage our broad diversity of people, global network and learnings
- Two brains are better than one (most often)

AGILE
- Learn by doing, use version 1.0, 2.0, 3.0
- Act with a sense of urgency

THE CONSCIENCE WE FOLLOW

DO THE RIGHT THING
- Our values shape the conscience we follow
- Use our global scale for leadership and for good, for progress
- And when we make mistakes, own them, put them right, learn from them, and grow

© 2019 The Coca-Cola Company

You will have to decide how deeply you want to research a company. There will be some companies with loads of information. Other companies, especially privately held companies, may have little to glean from their websites. Some organizations may not have much Internet presence, at all. In this case, you will need to be creative.

I chose my old company, Coca-Cola for a specific reason: to demonstrate that research is complicated. If you are interviewing for a position with a large corporation, make sure you know what company and division the position falls under. An Account Manager position, for example, may be part of the Local Coca-Cola Bottling Company—a completely different company than the corporate headquarters. That means that doing research on Coca-Cola corporate in Atlanta, while informative, may not be totally relevant to your interview. You must continue to drill down to find the exact company. This is especially true if you are interviewing with a large, publicly traded, national or international company. Large regional companies may not be as bad, but you still should check.

During my career, I encountered a funny situation when I was the VP of sales for a subsidiary of Colgate Palmolive. We were a wholly owned division that was in the pet food business. I interviewed a regional candidate who had done an incredible amount of preparation with financials, mission statements, vision and value statements, and an unbelievable amount of data that he had brought with him (in a notebook similar to the kind I recommend assembling!). Unfortunately, the content was all about Colgate, and he had absolutely no knowledge of our division and what we did other than manufacture and sell pet food let alone how we were structured.

As a wholly owned division, we were definitely managed and controlled by Colgate. We still had our own separate mission statement, our own vision and values, and a list of strategic imperatives for the company. The candidate had no information on us but was unable to pivot in the interview. He continued to ask me about Colgate, rather than our company, and it made the interview quite cumbersome. My suggestion is to be creative. If there isn't much information online, think outside the box. He could have gone to a pet store and interviewed the owner about the company and products. I have used this idea with great success. While he was talented, he did not get the job.

All the research that you have completed and compiled in your binder, when available, will give you plenty of information that will allow you to formulate a list of questions that you can ask during the interview. There are some dos and don'ts about interview questions, but we will cover the topic in **Chapter 7**.

Company Mission Statements

Most companies have a Mission Statement. I always use company mission statements as the basis for an interview question. I usually ask my interviewer to tell me about their mission statement. Sometimes you get interesting answers. Company management teams work long and hard to wordsmith the perfect mission statement and may even check during the interview to see if you have read it, so definitely find it and add it to your notebook.

Vision and Values

Just like a company mission statement, a company's Vision and Values are very important to know before an interview. So many companies today use cause marketing visions to distinguish themselves from their competitors. It is critical that you know and understand a company's vision and the values they care about to support their vision. Bombas® Socks built their company by giving away a pair of socks for every pair sold. If you had an interview with them, you would want to make sure you understand the company's motivation in doing this and be ready to discuss it. Doing so only takes about 20 seconds by going to the "About Us" section of their website—it is that easy![3] Not doing your homework could cost you the job.

---

[3] https://shop.bombas.com/

Products and Services

While this tab may sound like a no-brainer, it is not always that simple because differentiation among goods and services can at times be unclear. Returning to the Coca-Cola example, Coca-Cola Corporate is different from Coca Cola USA. Coca Cola International is different, too, as is Coca Cola's Fountain division. Each of these entities specializes in different aspects of the Coca-Cola business. For instance, Coca Cola Enterprises® (CCE) is the Operations side of the business, making, selling, and distributing Coca Cola brands and is a completely different publicly traded company than the others listed above. It can be very confusing, so when you do your research, make sure you are focusing on the products and services that correspond to the entity listed in the job description. You don't want to be the individual who focused on Colgate Corporate when he was interviewing with a completely different division.

Employee expectations and desired behaviors

In today's post-Covid-19 world, this tab is very important to research. Employee expectations and desired behaviors are not always the easiest information to locate on public-facing websites, so do your best and if you can't find what you are looking for, add these to your list of questions for the interview. Covid-19 caused a tectonic shift in corporate culture and expectations, and although many workplaces have returned to "normal," the definition of "normal" varies. Many companies still allow at least some opportunities to work from home, wear more laid-back attire, or to join video teleconference calls.

If you are looking for a job that allows you to work from home, it will be very important to find out if the new opportunity requires you to commute to the office every day. Company websites can sometimes offer this information, but if not, try to reach out to a current employee or the HR hiring manager. Ask questions, but I recommend being careful which questions you ask during the interview itself, particularly if you don't know the work culture, as your question may imply that you are not willing to work hard.

Organizational structure

This can be very difficult to obtain before an interview, but it is important to you from a career decision standpoint. When looking at the organizational structure, consider, for instance, if you will have opportunities for job growth. Some jobs earlier in your career might offer good experience with little headroom, so you know that if you are taking the job that you can expect to be back on the market in 2 to 3 years. Knowing these details may help you prepare for an interview question on why you want the job—in such cases it may be perfectly appropriate to say that you are looking to develop a particular skill before transitioning to a long-term position. Alternatively, if you had NOT done this research and responded to the same question with a remark on long-term development, the hiring official may think you're not a good fit for the job based on the lack of long-term opportunities that the position offers.

During my previous interview preparations if I had been unable to find a copy of the organizational chart, I always put a blank piece of paper in this tab and added "Organizational Structure" to my list of questions for the interview. Then, when I asked the question, I flipped to this tab and started taking notes while the hiring manager was talking. It helps to ask this question early in the interview, as it may affect how you craft some of your own interview responses.

Questions

Developing a list of questions is a critical part of your interview preparation and the Questions tab is a "must-have" in your interview notebook. We will dig deeper into the types of questions you might want to ask in **Chapter 7**. The great news is that once you have developed your list of questions for one job interview, they won't change significantly, so you will only need to tweak the list a bit if you interview with a different company.

Note Pages

This tab is very simple, but very critical. Whenever you are interviewing, you should always take notes. Having this tab makes things easy. All you do is fill this tab with about 10 pages of blank paper. When the interview starts, one of the first things you should do is ask permission to take notes. It is a sign of courtesy and respect and will score you points with the interviewer. In addition, the act of taking notes conveys your sense of purpose, commitment to the process, and attention to detail in a subtle, but impactful way.

Whenever possible, it is also helpful to write the interview questions down. This can keep you focused when you are responding so that you avoid rambling and make sure to answer every part of a question that is asked. I have served on some panel interviews where there were good candidates who did not ultimately get the job because they lost points by not answering all the questions asked. It's okay to have the interviewer repeat the question, and the act of writing the question down also gives you some "top cover" while you are formulating your response in your head.

Resumes

An interviewing best practice is to always stock four to five fresh copies of your resume in your interview binder, just in case! Many times, during interviews, an additional person from the company might "pop in" for a minute or for the whole interview. It is always nice to be able to offer the new participant a copy of your resume in case they have not seen one. Separately, having a copy of your resume in front of you during the interview, particularly if by phone, can be a quick reference point for you to glance at to prompt your memory during a question.

Interview story #5

A recruiter told me this story. Beware of your surroundings before, during, and after you have an interview. The CEO of a family-owned business was obsessed with cleanliness. He told the receptionist to listen to see if job applicants that used the restroom while they were waiting to be interviewed washed their hands after using the facilities. She would listen for the sink and towel dispenser and then report back to the CEO. He also asked the receptionist to score the applicants on their friendliness, professionalism, and communication skills. The receptionist also was to observe how the candidates waited. Did they sit upright and study their notes? Or were they slouching or staring at their phone?

Moral of the story: Remember, you are always on. From the moment you leave your car, you need to have your game face on and be observant of everyone you meet. You might just run into a curious CEO who happens to wander through the lobby to check you out. It happened to me. It can happen to you!

Chapter 6

Leveraging the Job Description

If you are not willing to learn, no one can help you. If you are determined to learn, no one can stop you.
—Zig Ziglar.

When I used to read a typical job description, my eyes tended to roll back in my head. Job descriptions can be overwhelming, bureaucratic, and complicated, and my first thought usually was "I'm not qualified." Once I had experienced hiring from the opposite side of the desk and understood the process better, including job descriptions, they no longer bothered me.

Here is the key to job descriptions. Typically, the department head or hiring manager usually initiates the process of recruiting to fill a new or existing position. Generally, they will send a request to someone in staffing within the HR department. With larger companies, they may already have an existing job description for the position. If not, the hiring manager will rarely actually create the job description. That task

41

usually falls on the HR department. The HR department wears many hats in an organization. They do not always get the best direction from the hiring manager on the key skills and strengths that the candidate is required to have for the job, so they improvise. They do this by adding skills and attributes that most positions need. In many cases, they add so many things that the job description looks like only someone with superhuman skills or powers will fill it. It is okay, do not panic! Look deeper at what the job description is saying.

There will be a list of soft skills and hard skills on most job descriptions. In **Chapter 1**, I discussed the three things that companies are focused on during a job search. Can the candidate do the job; will the candidate do the job; and will the candidate fit into our culture? The characteristics associated with these questions can show up in a job description. As far as "Can you do the job" goes, hiring managers look first at hard skills. Hard skills are the ones that can, and will, knock you out of the candidate pool immediately if you lack them. For instance, if you cannot speak fluent French and it is a hard, required skill, do not apply for the job. If you are not okay with lifting 50 pounds or being on your feet for 12 hours at a time, do not apply. If you are not familiar with Splunk or other types of platforms and the job requires it, don't apply. You get the picture. If you measure up to or are okay with the hard skills required, then spend time looking through the job description for the soft skills. Soft skills are focused on the attributes we discussed and explored in **Chapter 1**.

Here are some soft skill requirements that I observed in several recent job postings:

1. Creative: we are an out of the box thinking company and always innovating, we need this position to be filled with someone who can think out of the box.

2. Build execution capabilities to support the strategy, including developing talent maps or plans, workforce plans, competencies, know-ledge base, and go-to-market strategy with Business Development.

3. Recommend budgets to management, including staff utilization, technology, facility and equipment requirements or improvements.

4. Engage with prospective clients and follow best practices for B2B sales.

5. Manage a pipeline and perform proper follow up procedures.

6. Exceed sales goals as established by the organization.

7. Preparation of timely and accurate solution proposals.

8. Highly developed self-motivation skills and ability to work remotely with a cross functional matrixed team.

9. Run training meetings.

10. Prospect and contact potential customers using our long-used system.

Every Job description is going to list responsibilities somewhere on the page. The list may be short, or it may be incredibly long. It does not matter: the key is to isolate the skill or attribute that the company is looking for. Let's go back through that list of 10 and see what we find.

1. **Creative**: we are an **out of the box thinking** company and always **innovating**, we need this position to be filled with someone who can think out of the box.

2. **Build execution capabilities** to support the strategy including **developing talent** maps/plans, workforce plans, competencies, knowledge base and go-to-market strategy with Business Development.

3. **Recommend budgets to management**, including staff utilization, technology, facility and equipment requirements or improvements.

4. **Engage with prospective clients** and follow best practices for B2B sales.

5. **Manage a pipeline** and perform proper follow up procedures.

6. **Exceed sales goals** as established by the organization.

7. Preparation of timely and **accurate solution proposals.**

8. Highly developed **self-motivation skills** and ability to **work remotely** with a cross functional matrixed team.

9. **Run training meetings.**

10. **Prospect and contact potential customers** using our long-used system.

The bolded and underlined phrases condense the lists down to the key skills and attributes that each of these companies might value. Breaking down the job description in this way provides an excellent way to choose the skills and talents that you would plan to highlight with your personal stories during the interview. Every Job description will give you the key skill areas. In many cases, the most important skills are listed first, but not always.

One additional tip on job descriptions goes back to those job descriptions where you encounter a hard skill that you don't have. I used to keep a folder on my desktop titled "Dream Jobs," where I would file away those positions that I was interested in, but for which I lacked key qualifications. I would go through and highlight "reach skills" that I wanted to work on over time so that eventually those positions might turn into a realistic job opportunity. Some of these skills might be things that your current position does not develop, so you may have to be creative in finding ways to develop. For instance, you can take a class after work, but if you lack the funds, you might even consider "moonlighting" in a volunteer position or job that will develop a certain skill over time.

Interview story #6

This story begins after I have been through four interviews with a large, multi-national company. The recruiter called me and said that the Chief Operating Officer of the company was returning from a week out of the country and had a layover at Atlanta Airport. He had grabbed a suite at a nearby hotel and asked me to meet him there on a Sunday. This was unusual, but I decided to go with the flow. I suited up in my starched shirt and silk tie and headed out. I called his room, and he came down to meet me. He was in a golf shirt, shorts, and flip flops. He said "oh I forgot to tell you we were going to watch the last day of the Masters Golf Tournament today. You didn't need to wear a suit. Feel free to take off your tie and jacket. I went up to the suite and he had a spread of food and beers, and I spent the next 5 hours watching golf. Apparently, the position I was interviewing for required a lot of entertaining and he wanted to see how I interacted with him in a casual situation.

Moral of the story: Always look your best for an interview. You can always dress down if it is offered. Be ready to be flexible. You never know what a company might do in an interview.

Chapter 7

Developing Questions

The art and science of asking questions
is the source of all knowledge.
-Thomas Berger

Asking questions in an interview is paramount. First, it shows you are interested in learning more about the job, the company, and even the interviewer! Second, it enables you to learn as much as possible so you can feel comfortable that YOU want to go to the next step and ask for the job.

Developing your questions is an evolving process. The good news is that many of the questions you develop and add to your interview notebook can be used at every interview. There will always be questions that will be company- and job-specific that will require you to do some hard work before the interview. Developing more generic questions up front with simplify the process. Below, in no particular order, is a list of the typical categories that your question might fall into:

1. Questions about the interviewer
2. Questions about the company
3. Questions about the job
4. Questions about the company's commitment to training and personal development
5. Questions about the company's structure
6. Questions about the team that you will be joining
7. Questions about key performance indicators, goals, and personal success measurements
8. Questions about the company's culture

As I mentioned in **Chapter 5**, a tremendous amount of information can be found on company websites. In many cases, you can find a lot of basic information on the job description itself, from benefits, vacation days, to insurance allowances and more. That is why you should not take up valuable time in the interview to ask questions about these topics. While they are important, the interview is not the time to ask them.

Do not ask about vacation days in an interview, period! You may scratch your head, or even dismiss me for saying this, but it is a huge faux pas. Nor do you want to ask about the typical number of hours you will be expected to work each day. The reason that I bring it up is because it happens more often than you might imagine. There is a time and place to ask these very legitimate questions, but the interview is not the time. The time to ask it is AFTER, and ONLY after, you have received an offer. Your questions during the interview process must center around the company, its goals and aspirations, and questions about your own personal development and career growth.

Your questions should fall into the categories above. You can use the questions you ask as a way of demonstrating that you have done your research, but also be careful to avoid questions that demonstrate that you have NOT done your research. For instance, instead of simply asking the interviewer to talk about the company's mission statement (something that is clearly articulated on the company website), you could say something like "I noticed that the XYZ Company's mission statement is to [fill in the blank], but I wondered if you might be able to speak more on how your team fits into this mission." Knowing the answer might also help you determine if this is the right position for you.

The most important questions that you will ask will take place as the interviewer is wrapping things up. We will cover that in more depth in **Chapter 10, Closing the Interview**.

Interview Story #7

When conducting a job search you must be focused and aggressive. I found a job posting for a Vice President/General Manager position that I felt was the perfect role for me. In reading through the posting, I saw that they requested that all resumes be sent to a person at the company, and they gave her name and email address. I saw this as a huge opportunity, so I emailed her my resume and immediately followed that up with a phone call. When she answered the call, I introduced myself and let her know that I had just sent her my resume. She said she had received it but that she already had 25 qualified candidates and She wasn't taking any more resumes. I convinced her to add my resume to the pile, which she ultimately did. She mentioned that her boss (the CEO) was out of town and would be looking over everyone's resumes when he returned. I called her the next day and thanked her for adding me to the pile. We developed a bit of a rapport, so I asked her to put my resume at the top of the stack. She laughed and said, "wow, you really want this interview." This resulted not only in getting the interview; I also got the job!

Moral of the story: Being aggressive and creative is a must for job seekers. You cannot expect anyone to advocate for you other than yourself, which means that you'll need, at times, to step outside your comfort zone and be bold. Fight hard to get recognized by companies. It will pay off!

Chapter 8

Interview types, strategies, and pitfalls

Strategy is about setting yourself apart from the competition. It's not a matter of being better at what you do – it's a matter of being different at what you do.
— **Michael Porter**

As I mentioned at the beginning of this manual, a company is generally looking to answer three questions about a candidate during the interview process. Those questions are:

1. Can you do the job?
2. Will you do the job?
3. Will you fit in to our culture?

These three questions will be the driving force behind the questions that a company will develop to determine if the candidate is the right choice. They will seek to determine this throughout every facet of the process, from the job application, your resume and cover letter, your interviews, and potentially one or more personality profile or aptitude tests. Obviously the longer you have been in the workplace, the easier it will be to determine the first key point from your resume. Having less experience is okay, but it just requires the company to rely more on soft skills. Every interview will involve questions about both **Hard Skills** and **Soft Skills**. You need to be ready to answer both.

If you look over the next few pages, you will see examples of soft skills I have laid out for the three major interest areas that a company might have in you. It is by no means the only soft skills they might look for, but it will give you a feel of the types of skills that fall into each area.

As you are preparing and building your skills inventory, I suggest that you categorize your skills into these three areas to give you a better picture of the value you bring to potential companies.

Can you do the Job?

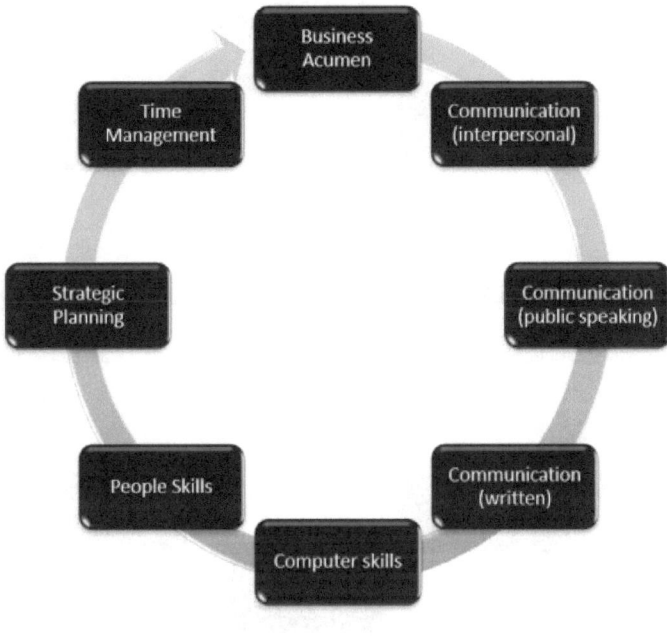

Some of the skills companies may look for in a candidate to determine if the candidate can do the job.

Will you do the job?

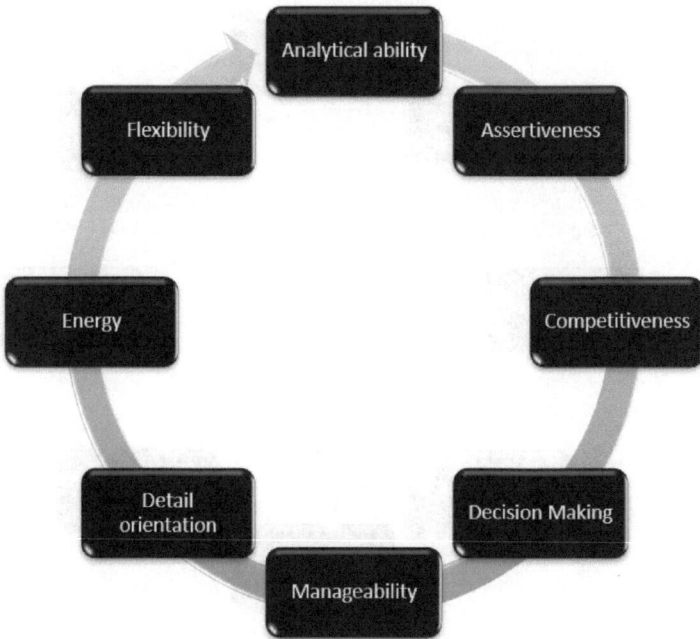

Some of the skills companies may
look for in a candidate to determine
if the candidate will do the job.

WILL YOU FIT THE COMPANY CULTURE?

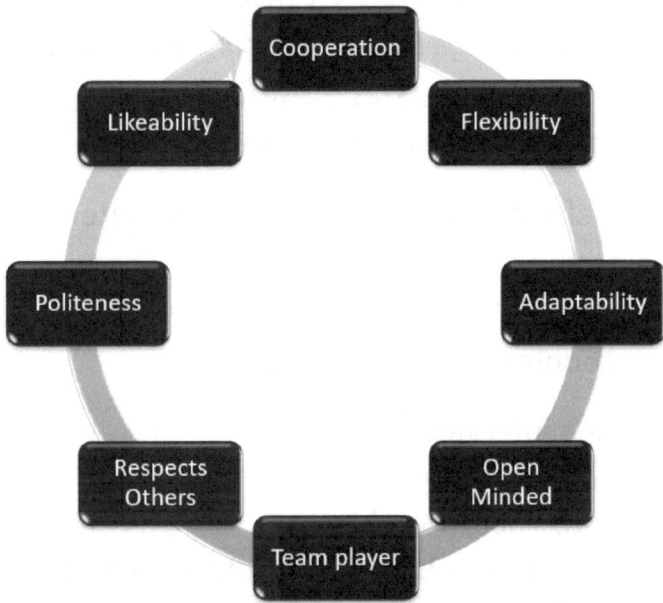

Companies want to get to the CORE of your motivation:

Why are you here?

What do you want?

Where do you want to go with your life?

Where do you want to be in a year? Three years? Five years?

Note: *To be clear, Hard Skills are technical skills. Proficiency in Programming languages, foreign languages, Forklift Driving certificates. Commercial Driver's License (CDL) etc. Soft Skills focus on things like leadership, Motivational skills, Organizational skills, positive attitude etc. These are the skills you wrote stories about.*

To refresh your memory from **Chapter 3**, below are the types of interviews that you may encounter. Every company is different, so you may encounter some or all of these:

Phone interviews
Zoom interviews
Fact-to-Face interviews
Team interviews (multiple interviewees)
Panel interviews (multiple interviewers)
Peer interviews
Personality or IQ profile testing
"Rubber Stamp" interviews
Interview Questions

Phone Interviews and Zoom Interviews

Phone interviews are still the most common first contact during the interviewing process. Virtual Interviewing has become more common, especially following the Covid-19 Pandemic. There are things that you can do to help your cause when faced with a phone or Zoom interview. As usual, preparation and organization are key to a successful outcome.

A KEY POINT TO REMEMBER IS: THESE INTERVIEWS ARE HAPPENING TO TRIM DOWN THE LIST OF APPLICANTS. THE GOAL THAT YOU SHOULD HAVE FOR THESE IS TO MAKE THE CUT AND LAND ANOTHER INTERVIEW.

The operative word for phone and Zoom interview calls is ENTHUSIASM. Your attitude during these types of interviews is especially critical as the feedback for the interviewer is limited compared to a face-to-face interview. The interviewer will be able to sense your enthusiasm through the phone and on a Zoom call. Since the objective of the interviewer is to reduce the number of applicants, being positive and upbeat is the foundation for your discussion.

Clock

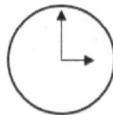

Smile

Monitor & Camera	

Enthusiasm

My Research Notebook	My Questions	Specific Company Research
Bullet List My Stories by attribute	Tablet for Note Taking	My Resume

My Workspace or Desktop

Organizing Your Desktop For
Phone or Video Interviews

Here is a tip: Make a sign or sticky note with the word ENTHUSIASM and place it in your direct line of sight when you are on the phone. It will remind you to stay positive throughout the call. Also, make a sign or sticky note that says SMILE with a smiley face. Remembering to smile is not as easy as it sounds, especially when you are focused on providing a compelling answer to an interviewer's question. The University of Portsmouth conducted a study that documented that someone can HEAR your smile.[4] It has to do with the muscles in your face, but the key takeaway for our purposes is that your physical emotions and expressions while you are talking will be translated even if the interview is not face-to-face.

So once your signs or sticky notes are in place, you need to organize your desk. Start with a clear workspace. Since your interview will probably be 20 to 30 minutes, you will need to be extremely focused and precise with what you say, how you say it, and to effectively use the time you have been given. I would encourage you to have a clock on your desk or workspace so that you are always aware of the time. There are six key things that I recommend you lay out in your workspace:

1. **Your Research Notebook**. Always keep this handy. If you are on a video call it is okay to show them how you are organized.

2. **Your Questions**: Keep your interview questions front and center. You will want to be prepared to ask them succinctly to keep the interview flowing, so it is important to take the key questions that you would like

---

[4] NPR, "Hearing a Smile in tone of Voice," Weekend Edition Saturday. January 19, 2008. Accessed online November 19, 2023 at: https://www.npr.org/templates/story/story.php?storyId=18255131

to ask and write them out on a separate piece of paper for this interview.

3. **Company Research:** Keep copies of any research that you have found on the company in case you need to refer to it during the conversation. It may be used in conjunction with one of your questions. For example, you could say "In researching your company, I found this quote on your website about your vision" (You would reach over to your pile of research and pull it out).

4. **Resumes**: Always keep a copy close in case the interviewer asks you a specific question about an item on your resume. Then you have it handy to pick up and reference.

5. **Tablet for notes**: Whenever the interviewer is talking, make sure to write down any key points they are making. Especially if they are answering a question that you have asked. This is valuable to have so that you can respond when needed. Make sure to write down the questions they ask. That way you can make sure that you answer every part of their question when telling a story or providing a response.

6. **Your List of Stories**:   Keep your stories (written long hand or typed out) so you can look at them when you are providing an example of one of your skills. It will help you to remember key points to make when you are talking. You may wish to include a shorter bulletized version for quick reference.

Lighting and sound are very important elements for video interviews. You should get comfortable with the microphone on your computer and test it with a friend before the call. If your computer microphone is not the best, you might consider an external microphone. There are many options at Walmart ®or on Amazon®. The same goes for your lighting. Just make sure that your camera is putting you in the best possible light (no pun intended). There are some inexpensive lighting options available if you would like to add light to your desk.

Every day I hear more and more companies using a video-based screening process to knock out candidates that do not fit their profile. The most typical format involves emailing the candidate with a link once the application is received. The link takes the candidate to a landing page that explains the process for the video interview. Typically, a candidate will be administered anywhere from five to ten questions in succession. You will be asked to read the question and take 30 to 60 seconds to formulate your answer. When you are ready, you click on the record button and record your answer. Some companies offer you the opportunity to review your answer and if you would like, do a second or third take. Other companies just give you one shot. Pure and simple, these are screening interviews. With preparation, you will have a significant advantage over those applicants that just "wing it."

Face-to-Face interviews

These can take many forms and locations from a coffee shop to an office building. I have had interviews over breakfast, lunch, and dinner. I have had interviews in hotel suites and bars. It all depends on the company and their style, along with the interviewer and their schedule. If you have followed my steps during the past few chapters, you will be more than prepared to conduct the interview properly.

One tip that I have used with solid results is to try to find out the name of the person you will be meeting with for your interview. It isn't always possible, but it is important to try to find out before your interview. The reason is because you might be able to locate a formal biography or resume on the company or organization's website, or the person may have a LinkedIn profile. Print that biography, resume, or profile out and add it to the research tab in your job search notebook. Study it: find out where they have worked prior to their current job, where they went to school, what fraternity, or sorority they were in, etc. All this information can be incredibly helpful when it comes to the time for the interview. It is important to always remember that an interview is a conversation, not an inquisition. It is okay for you to ask questions and you should be prepared to do so. I will discuss this more in-depth in the next chapter.

Regarding interviews that occur over a meal, I recommend that you order something simple like oatmeal for breakfast, and salad for lunch or dinner—and then do not eat it! You can push it around your plate and maybe take one bite, but let it go. There is too much that can go wrong. My Hamburger story is the best example.

Team Interviews

Team interviews are less common but may be used during preliminary screening calls or for interviews for schools or colleges. Broadly speaking, a group of up to 5 to 7 candidates will be assembled to answer several questions. Each candidate is given the brief opportunity to respond, in most cases with very short responses. Candidates may be required to provide a one-word response to the same question (such that if you are the last to respond you have more time to think through your response), or alternatively, each candidate may be asked to answer a different question in a round robin style. This interview method is focused less on your actual response, and more on your demeanor, personality, and professionalism, so don't overthink your responses. Do you stand out from the crowd? It's important to stay positive and make sure to listen carefully and stay engaged while others are responding.

Panel Interviews

Panel Interviews are very common in the modern workforce. The idea is simple: the hiring manager would like to canvas several people's opinions on the candidate. Usually, the team chooses behavioral-based interview questions. Typically, the questions will be chosen in advance and each interviewer with have their assigned questions. While one person asks the question and engages with the interviewee, the other two team members will be observing the body language of the candidate and taking notes on the completeness and quality of the answer. Typically, one of the people on the panel will be the lead interviewer. They will control the process for the duration of the interview. You should direct initial questions to that person. As the interview progresses, direct your answers primarily to the person who asks the question. It will show confidence if you make eye contact with all panelists as you answer but focus primarily on the person that asked the question.

Peer interviews

This method of interviewing is a bit more unusual but should be treated like any other interview. It is important to note that while the interviewer may be introduced to you as a potential peer, you should not relax or let your guard down. Remember "You are always on." Your answers should be as crisp and direct as they would be with a hiring manager. They are generally looking for "fit" in this kind of interview, so being a team player goes a long way. I recommend asking a lot of culture questions during a peer interview. Get them talking about what it is like to work at the company. What attracted them? What is their favorite part of their job, etc.? It is an opportunity to do some good research for yourself.

Personality Profile Testing

You may encounter a company that conducts personality profile tests prior to, during, or after an interview. Since these tests vary greatly, it is virtually impossible to provide coaching here. I do have one very specific thought about these types of tests. Do not over think them or try to guess what the company is trying to figure out about you. That could cause you to skew the results unfavorably. Just answer honestly and quickly. That method almost always generates the most accurate result. You are who you are. Either you are a fit or you are not. Don't sweat the tests.

"Rubber Stamp" interviews

As I mentioned in my Hamburger story, "Rubber Stamp" interviews can be tricky and very dangerous. The basic premise is that the hiring manager has chosen you as the final candidate and plans to make you a job offer. As a courtesy to his or her boss, they thought it might be nice for you to meet their boss, or another member of the senior management team. BE CAREFUL. If you do not have a written job offer, you do not have the job. One mistake, false move, or lame comment could cause your ship to sink. Until you have a written offer you do not have a job!

Interview Questions

Every company and every interviewer have their own style, organization, and goals for their interviews. The Internet is full of lists of questions for interviews. Headlines include topics like "The 10 toughest Interview questions" or "the one question you must know for every interview." I am not a fan of memorizing answers to questions that may never get asked. Focusing on getting comfortable talking about YOUR skills and talents is a much better use of your time.

You never know how an interviewer may start the conversation. Many interviewers in today's "flatter" organizations may have been promoted to their managerial position based upon merit or performance in mission critical situations. Unfortunately, many managers do not get the proper training in interviewing, so their performance and predictability can vary greatly. If they ask more general questions, those are easier to answer. If they asked you what you would do if confronted by a particular situation, your answer would be hard to quantify because they really wouldn't know for sure if you would react that way. The classic "Tell Me about yourself" question is the way that most interviews start. I have an out of the box way that I deal with that question. I will discuss this in depth in the next chapter.

A newer approach to interviewing has emerged during the past couple of decades and includes focusing on behavioral-based Interview questions. Behavioral-based interview questions are generally one of the most frequently used types of questions for larger, more sophisticated companies, as their interviewing processes are usually more structured and defined. Larger companies usually have a team of human resource professionals working there and, generally, they have been highly trained in the recruiting process. Behavioral Interview questions are a more complete way to search out critical skills that the company is looking for in each position. These questions are typically asked to watch and explore how the candidate might act in a particular situation and what skills the candidate would employ to mitigate the problem presented in the question. There are literally hundreds of these questions, covering virtually every imaginable situation. To be effective in this type of structured question environment, you will need to rely on many of the skills and processes you worked on in earlier chapters of this book.

Knowing your strongest attributes and skills will give you a huge advantage. Understanding how to use the S.T.A.R. format to structure and present you answers will make a strong impact on the interviewer as many people, when under pressure to respond effectively to a difficult question have a tendance to ramble and get lost in their own answer. S.T.A.R. helps you avoid that. Aggressively scouring the job description to identify key attributes that the position requires will pay dividends as well. You can bet that the behavioral questions will most likely be structured around situations where you have exhibited the desired skills in the past. To learn how you might perform in the future requires them to examine how you have acted in the past.

While responding to questions, you should also expect to be interrupted by the interviewer, who might want you to expand on a statement that you made. Remember, they are asking the question so they can uncover specific things. Do be distracted by that, it is part of the process. Keeping track of where your story is in the S.T.A.R. format will allow you to keep moving on to the conclusion of the story without getting lost.

The format of a Behavioral Interview Question can start with a hypothetical situation and set up a challenge that someone might have to face. It could start something like this:

"Can you tell me about a time when" and then adds the situation that the interviewer must respond to. There are so many scenarios that it is difficult to even try to capture them. The beauty of this type of question is best answered with a story. If you work hard on learning and perfecting the S.T.A.R. story format, you can respond to the question in a clear and concise manner. Here are a few examples of Behavioral Questions.

- Give me a specific example of a time when you used good judgment and logic in solving a problem.
- Give me an example of a time when you set a goal and were able to meet or achieve it.
- Tell me about a time when you had to use your presentation skills to influence someone's opinion.

When the question is asked, make sure you listen intently and take time to breathe and compose yourself before you answer. It is okay and normal. Interviewers expect and want you to take time to formulate your answer. If you have studied the job description and memorized stories about skills you have that they are looking for, this process will be much easier. By doing the work up front, your notebook will have many of the answers they are looking for. Most importantly, remember to smile and tell your stories with passion and enthusiasm. Have Fun!

Interviewer Story #8

This has only happened to me once, but you read about it all the time. Be truthful about your jobs and accomplishments. I had an interview with a candidate that was presented to me by a recruiter. I was told this guy was the real deal and he had a resume to back it up. Sure enough, the interview went incredibly well. The guy was a great communicator and had strong answers to each of my questions. This was before the Internet or social media, so we only had references to verify people's employment etc. When the interview ended, I was very impressed. I called the recruiter and expressed my delight with the candidate. I asked him how his references checked out and he said he was only able to connect with one of the references and it was positive. I wanted a little more comfort before I made an offer so on a whim, I ask the recruiter to call the University of Georgia the verify his degree. That's when things began to unravel. He had never attended UGA. The recruiter dug deeper and found that he had not worked for any of the companies on his resume. The candidate was certainly charismatic, but he was a total con!

Moral of the story: Be truthful! In today's world of instant search results, everything is discoverable. Google can (and will!) find things. Companies regularly fact check many things when researching a candidate. Make sure everything you put on your resume is accurate and irrefutable.

Chapter 9

Face to face Interviews

It's hard to say exactly what it is about face-to-face contact that makes deals happen, but whatever it is, it hasn't yet been duplicated by technology.
- Paul Graham

Face-to-face interviews are the point in the hiring process that everyone is striving for and where your skills get put to the test. First, congratulate yourself on making it to this point! In some cases, this means that you've made it past electronic screening of hundreds of applications, and perhaps an initial phone interview with human resources. Either way, it is not an easy task, so it is a win.

While each face-to-face interview will be different, the one thing you will be able to control is your own presentation and demeanor. Here are some things to consider before you arrive at your interview location:

1. **What to wear**: In today's 21st century work environment, this is a challenging question. Many companies today, especially in the tech industry, are very casual. Tee shirts, jeans, and flip-flops may be the typical garb for an office. My recommendation here is to tread carefully (literally!). I am a big fan of being overdressed for an interview. If the work environment is "business casual," ladies should dress professionally with a suit combination (jacket, blouse, and pants or skirt). A nice sweater set, and pants are also great. Men should wear a tie and sport coat.

   If the environment is casual, a sport coat and collared shirt would be great. Remember not to remove your jacket unless encouraged to do so by your interviewer. Do your homework. If you receive no instructions and are worried, you might also consider reaching out to someone on LinkedIn® that works for the company to see if they will give you some tips or recommendations. Find their office and go check out the environment. On the day of the interview, skip the cologne or perfume— you don't want to do anything that attracts attention away from your interview responses or leaves a bad memory!

2. **Location**: Even with today's technology with GPS maps for your phone and precise arrival time estimates, it is a good idea to find out exactly where you are going. First, map the location on your computer or phone. If it looks straight forward, simply send the map link or linked address to yourself to use on the day of your interview. You may, however, wish to conduct a dry run. This will eliminate doubt and stress on the big day and will enable you to focus on what you will say. I recently had to go to a meeting that was in a complex of office buildings. Each building was locked and required someone to buzz you in. It took me 30 minutes to figure out which door was the right door and I walked what seemed to be about a mile in the process. Knowing where you are going takes the pressure off. Plan to arrive 30 minutes before your allotted time.

3. **Entering the office**: I had a saying in business, which is that **"YOU ARE ALWAYS ON."** Remember that from the moment you step out of your car, the game is on! You need to put a big smile on your face and have a spring in your step. From the moment you enter the office for your interview, your senses need to be on full alert. If there is a receptionist, greet them with a smile and a positive "hello." Let them know who you are and with whom you are meeting.

If you are asked to take a seat, sit on the edge of the seat. Do not slouch in the chair. The receptionist or another employee may be charged with watching you to see how you act (remember the Cleanliness CEO!). I was once waiting for an interview with a company's Senior Vice President. As I sat in the reception area, the CEO walked by and stopped to introduce himself to me. He knew I was coming in and wanted to check me out. I was glad I had been sitting up straight, attentively studying my notebook.

4. **Body Language:** Your body language can say a lot in an interview. From the moment the interviewer walks up to you, you should be tuned into both your body language and theirs. Make eye contact with them and give the interviewer a strong handshake. When you sit, sit on the edge of the chair with your back straight with both feet firmly on the floor together. As the conversation begins, open your notebook to the tab for notes and be ready to take notes when needed. All these movements convey confidence and positivity. Remember that good eye contact is critical to effective conversations. Whenever you are talking, make sure to look the interviewer right in the eyes and smile. If you are interviewing with a panel, you may focus primarily on the

person who asked a specific question, but make sure you make eye contact with each of the panelists.

5. **Starting the Interview:** A large percentage of interviews begin with the interviewer asking the age-old question; "So, can you tell me about yourself?" Most candidates are ready for this and begin telling the interviewer about themselves. Some start with their education, some start with where they were born or where they grew up. The answers vary as much as the candidates. I have a problem with this because an interview, when properly completed, is a conversation between two people. It is not a one-sided inquisition. I encourage the people I coach to answer this broad general question by asking two quick questions of their own. There is an adage in sales that "whoever is asking the questions is controlling the conversation." It is for that reason that I suggest jumping right in with your own questions right off the bat. This establishes the fact that you are ready to have a discussion, it will also help you if you are a bit nervous. I recommend asking the following two questions in a very conversational way:

a. *Is the position you are seeking to fill a new position or is the position vacant due to a promotion or a termination?*

b. *If the perfect candidate was to walk through this door, what might they look like?*

Here is how it might sound conversationally:

Hiring Manager: "So can you tell me a about yourself"?

Candidate: "Absolutely, I would be happy to but I was wondering if it might be okay to ask you a couple of questions before I start?"

Hiring Manager: "Sure go ahead."

Candidate: "I was curious about this position. Is the position you are seeking to fill a new position or is the position vacant due to a promotion or a termination?

Hiring Manager: "This position became vacant when we promoted the incumbent to a new role."

Candidate: "Wow, that is good to know! My

80

second question is a little different: if the perfect candidate were to walk through this door, what might they look like?"

Hiring Manager: "The perfect candidate would have to be..."

They would then list the key attributes that they are looking for in a great candidate. As they talk, write down the key points that you will need to address when you start talking about yourself and the skills and attributes you would bring to the company. If they are looking for a leader, make sure to work in a story you have memorized about your leadership skills.

In most interviews, it will play out something like the conversation above. That is not always the case, though, so do not be surprised or disappointed if they don't respond positively. One person that I was working with tried this tactic and the hiring manager surprised her with a very terse response. He told her "I am the CEO; I ask the questions and you answer them so please tell me about yourself." She was surprised and soldiered on.

The interesting thing was that by getting her question in right off the bat, she learned something very important. She was concerned that if his demeanor was that dictatorial to her as a job candidate, how badly would he treat her as an actual employee. She realized she would never have been happy working for him. She decided at that very moment that she was no longer interested in the job. Questions always generate information that will help you in many ways, regardless of the information they generate. Great interviews are filled with questions from both sides of the table. Just make sure you don't forget to answer all question components, as you may be leaving "points" on the table.

6. **Hard questions:** Interviews can go in many directions. It is impossible to predict them but at some point, more difficult questions may arise. If your resume or job history has holes or gaps, you will almost always get asked about these unaccounted-for periods of time. The truth is always the best recipe. Be honest and explain exactly why the gap occurred. In today's post Covid-19 world, gaps are common.

I remember working with one candidate who was worried because he did not have a computer science degree from college and had taught himself programming skills and languages. He was concerned that this might make him a less competitive job applicant. I encouraged him to be proud of the fact that he had taught himself and not worry about it. When he went to the interview, one of the first questions he was asked was "Son, where did you get your computer science degree?" He responded, "Well Sir, I actually taught myself." The interviewer's response was unexpected but positive. He said, "That's great! We prefer self-taught programmers over the degreed programmers. They seem to hit the ground running a lot faster." The good news is that by telling the truth, he got the job!

Another difficult question that seems to come up frequently during interviews (I am not a fan!) is "Tell me about your biggest weakness." We all have strengths and weaknesses. We are human, of course! Why some interviewers like this question, I will never know, but it is best to prepare for it. My advice is to simply be honest. The important thing is to not only share what you feel is a weakness but also share what steps you are taking to mitigate or to improve this weakness. Your interviewer will likely be observing your self-awareness, your honesty, how you characterize these weaknesses, and how you compensate. A lot of people recommend selecting something like "I am impatient," because by being impatient, this suggests that you are a "go-getter." But this is not a good answer, please do avoid this response because the interviewer will mostly be thinking of the potential negative effects of impatience, like poor interpersonal skills, or shoddy or rushed output.

7. **Engaging the interviewer:** Remember, you are interviewing the company just as much as they are interviewing you, so engaging the interviewer with questions is a good thing. You do not have to wait until they ask you if you have any questions before you can ask them. If the interviewer makes a statement about the company or position that you would like to explore, ask! Say something like "that's interesting can you tell me more about that?" By asking questions and looking for more information, the interview becomes more conversational. It also allows you to observe the interviewer. Just be conscious of time, as

the interviewer may have a set number of questions to get through in a given period of time.

Interviewer Story #9

I was once interviewing graduating seniors for entry-level positions at a major southern university. I had a full schedule with candidates every 45 minutes for 8 hours. My 9:00 AM interview had just concluded, and my next student was late. After about 15 minutes I was ready to give up on him when the door sprung open and in, he came, huffing and puffing from a run across campus to get here. Apparently, he had been in a final exam, and it had taken longer than he had thought so he had had to run to get there. The problem was that in April, in the south, it is quite hot and humid, so by the time he arrived he was soaking wet and burning up in his tweed sport coat. He slumped down in his chair still panting, with sweat running down his face. He felt compelled to rip off his coat as if he were on fire. Then, I had the distinct honor of a front row seat to his drenched blue shirt and silk tie. He wasn't getting any cooler, so the tie had to come off as well. Now, we hadn't said so much as a "hello" and his jacket and tie were off, and the first three buttons of his shirt were undone. I couldn't help but wonder if the pants were next. He finally caught his breath, and we exchanged a few questions and he left. He wasn't asked back. What should he have done?

Moral of the story: As I have said before, planning saves a lot of headaches. Schedule your interviews with plenty of time to arrive. In this case, telling the truth and just asking if it was possible to reschedule the interview would have been much better.

Chapter 10

Closing the Interview

All our dreams can come true
if we have the courage to pursue them.
— Walt Disney.

Closing the interview is a crucial step in the interview process. At some point in every interview, the interviewer decides that it is time to wrap up the discussion. They may need to leave for a meeting or get ready to meet the next candidate. Regardless of why, all interviews come to this critical point where the interviewer might say something like: "well Peter, I have really enjoyed our conversation today. Do you have any other questions for me?"

If you have been following the steps listed in the previous chapters, you have already asked several pertinent questions and done your research. Instead of asking for additional job-related details, you can use this time to ask a couple of process questions. Before you do this, I highly recommend that you develop and use what I call your "Closing Remarks."

As a former salesperson, I view the concept of "Closing Remarks" as parallel to the critical part of a sales call where you "Ask for The Order." Great salespeople are great closers and there is a real art to closing. Asking for the order essentially entails eliminating any lingering doubts that a buyer might have that your product is the correct choice.

Some people I have interviewed have taken a very direct approach at this point in the interview, asking me something like "So, how do you think I did?" or "Do you think I have the necessary skills for this job?" Although I admire the fortitude of someone who can ask an interviewer a question like that, it is not the best use of your last few minutes of the interview. Most interviewers will not answer such a question directly, whether out of fairness considerations for other candidates or perhaps because they may want to review all the components of the interview process before making a decision. Asking so directly will probably make some interviewers uncomfortable, which is the very last sentiment you want them to associate with you when they are considering the final offer.

Instead, I have found I found it better to present my closing remarks and then ask a few process questions. It's a bit like acting and takes practice. The more that you can tailor your remarks to the position, the better. Keep in mind that your goal is always getting to the next step. Here is how I might respond to the Interviewer:

Interviewer: So, Peter, I really enjoyed our conversation today. I need to get to another meeting, so I just wanted to see if you had any other questions for me.

Peter: Mr. Interviewer, thank you so much for your time. After researching your company (Hold up your notebook here to emphasize your preparation and organizational skills), I was excited to have the opportunity to meet with you today. Everything I have found about your company and the job so far suggests that it's the perfect fit for me. After talking with you today, I am even more excited about this opportunity. I really would like to continue our discussions and have a few short questions.

(Time for the process questions)

Question 1. What are the next steps that you will be going through to fill the position?

Question 2. What is the timeline to fill the position (days, weeks etc.)?

Question 3. Will you be making the final decision after you finish this round of interviews?

Question 4. Do you see me as one of the candidates that might make it to the next round? (or what are the qualifications you are looking for in the candidates who might make it to the next round?)

Now I know that I just said I don't normally like this latter type of question (**Question 4**), but have found that when it was asked after the preceding process questions, it seemed more logical to the interviewer and they were more forthcoming with an answer like "We will be having another round of interviews next week and I am confident that you will be one of the candidates."

BOOM! There is your answer. You made that cut. That was the goal: make it to the next round. Remember, the purpose of an interview is to get to the next round. Developing your "Closing Remarks" and memorizing them is important. By memorizing them, you can practice until it sounds like you are speaking extemporaneously when you are not. Eventually you will make it to the final interview that gets you the ultimate prize: a job offers. Keep in mind, however, that a job offer isn't "real" until you have a formal written offer in-hand.

The flip side of **Question 4** is that you must be careful what you wish for, because you might receive an answer like this: "well, we have a lot of candidates that we will be interviewing for this position so once we have completed this round of interviews, we will be letting the candidates know what the next steps are. This is a tricky answer. It can sometimes mean that you aren't getting a call back, but not always. If you get an answer like this one, take the opportunity to ask another question. I usually say, "Thanks for letting me know that. When do you think you will finish this round of interviews and when should I expect a call back?"

What do you do when applying for a position where the process is very clearly laid out? The closing remarks and process combination doesn't always work. There are times when if you've done your research, you should know exactly what the process is. Asking process questions in such cases may suggest that you haven't read the instructions and can backfire. In such cases, I would recommend including the closing remarks as planned, and adding a context question that can help you decide if you want the job.

As I have mentioned in an earlier chapter, the interview is just as much your opportunity to see if a job is a good fit for you as their opportunity to see if you're a good fit. You should feel free to include any questions in your closing remarks that will help you answer any lingering concerns that you might have. If you have done your research, you might have read the biography or resume of the person who is interviewing you, but you might choose to ask them a question like "what do you like most about working here?" It's a simple question but may give your insight into whether that person genuinely enjoys their work. Their response also might trigger a relevant thought, memory, or an experience that you've had that you could use for the next interview round.

The final step to closing the interview is sending a written follow-up thank you note to your interviewer. Depending on how your interview was conducted, you might be able to take one of your interviewer's business cards on the way out or write down their name and address. The best practice is to dash off a quick thank you card in the car as soon as you finish the interview. Don't wait until you get home, do it right in the parking lot. That way your card, when mailed, will be the first to arrive, since most everyone else will wait until they get home (you may even be able to drop it off at the security desk at the building's entrance). Most of the other candidates won't even bother to send one. It is a great way to put an exclamation point on your professionalism with the interviewer.

Negotiating a change to a job offer

Your leverage In the Interview Process

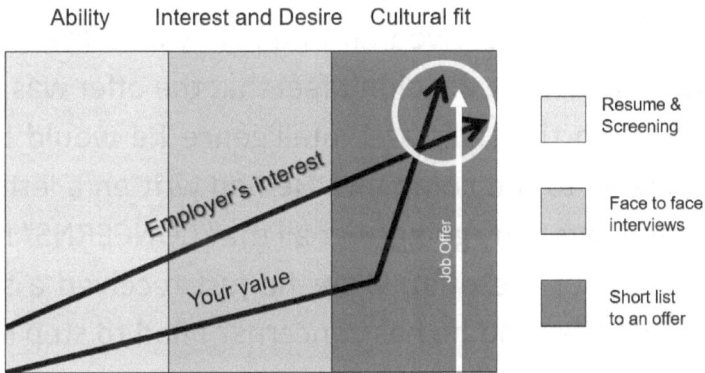

You can start negotiating once you get an offer! Not before

At last! You received an offer from the company! As you can see from the graph above, your value to the company rose steadily as you maneuvered through the interview process. The lines crossed and the offer arrives. What a relief. When you are reading through it, a couple of things are not as you expected. Now what do you do? You have invested so much time and energy in this process, let alone the emotional investment in getting this job. Do you try to negotiate or just take what they offered? That is the dilemma faced by many job applicants that get an offer. There is a fear that if you try to negotiate, they may rescind the offer. While that is certainly possible, it all depends on how you do it.

I was coaching a gentleman through an interview process he was going through with a massive multi-national company. He sailed through the process and received an offer. He called me and was very upset. He didn't feel that the offer was in line with the skills and intelligence he would be bringing to the company. He had written a letter to the company going over all the "CONCERNS" he had about the offer. Wow, he just received a six figure offer and he has concerns? I had to step in.

First of all, let's celebrate the fact that he received an offer. That means a lot of candidates didn't. So, let's start with the fact that he should not have "concerns." The way I like to approach this is with questions. I encouraged him to pass me the list of concerns that he had, and it really was only one serious concern: base pay.

My recommendation to him was to write an email back to the hiring manager expressing his gratitude for the offer emphasizing the fact that he was incredibly excited to start. I suggested that he use a very non-threatening statement to discuss the base salary question. He simply wrote that while he was grateful for the offer, he wanted to know if there was any flexibility in the base pay offered. He then listed a few reasons why he felt he deserved more. By taking this softer approach versus expressing concern, the company came back with a new offer that was $12,000 higher. He was thrilled and took the job on the spot.

I have had great success using this technique over the years. If they come back with a hard no, I always ask if there is an opportunity for a signing bonus. Many companies use this, and it is sometimes charged to a different line item in their budgets versus the salary line.

If all requests are rejected, then you have a decision to make. I always recommend trying to negotiate if you can, but gently and positively is the best method. Remember, they offered you the job, but usually there is another candidate who finished second and is eager to respond. Don't push too hard if you really want the job. They might just rescind your offer and go for the other candidate.

Interview story #10

I was interviewing for a temporary, lateral assignment at my job, and while a formal position description with job responsibilities had been posted online, I wasn't entirely clear on what they were looking for. I had gone through the interview preparation process, including closing remarks with a version of Question 4 (What are the qualifications you are looking for in the candidates who might make it to the next round?) that I had planned to ask at the end of the interview. When I walked in for my interview panel, they kicked the interview off by saying "Before we start, do you have any questions?" Without thinking about it, I asked, "Job description aside, are there key qualifications or characteristics that you are looking for in a candidate?" They answered, and as a result I was able to tailor my responses to their questions using stories that demonstrated those key characteristics. I got the job!

Moral of the Story: Be flexible! If you know your material backwards and forwards, you'll be better able to adjust on the fly. You may also need to use your judgment to adjust any questions or closing remarks based on what you hear during the interview.

Chapter 11

Social Media

The good thing about social media is it gives everyone a voice. The bad thing is...it gives everyone a voice.

- Brian Solis

Social Media is a global phenomenon that needs no introduction. There are so many options to interact socially online that it would be difficult to provide a truly comprehensive list. But there are several implications that social media has with respect to job interviews, and I will focus in this chapter on two platforms that I think are critical to the job seeker. Those two platforms are LinkedIn® and Facebook®.

LinkedIn

In today's world, LinkedIn is the place to be if you are working in any capacity. Originally designed to be a business social network, it has grown into what I call the world's largest job board. For the job seeker, LinkedIn provides a treasure trove of opportunities. Many companies post jobs on LinkedIn, so the platform can be a great place to look in addition to the company's website. More importantly, you can use the platform to search for companies' key executives or managers to reach out to for advice. It doesn't always work but you can always try. For this reason, creating and completing a LinkedIn profile is worth the effort during the job search process (and no, they are not sponsoring me to say this!).

Your LinkedIn profile is a critical thing to develop and curate as most companies will look you up on LinkedIn if you apply for a job. When creating your profile, be sure to include a high quality, professional headshot for your profile picture—this may be an employer's first and only impression of you before you meet during the interview. List your key attributes in your profile and make sure it is as complete as a professional resume, as it can be used when you apply for jobs via LinkedIn. Reach out to your connections and build your network. Unlike other social media platforms, make sure there is a good, *professional*, reason to connect and be careful not to accept connections with just anyone.

Checking social media, and LinkedIn in particular, has become one of the regular steps that most companies take during the recruiting process. They will be interested in how you have presented yourself. For example, they might want to observe whether your resumé and LinkedIn profile match, or even look at the size of your network.

Once your profile is complete it is very easy to start searching for jobs on LinkedIn. According to LinkedIn, below are the steps you would take to search for jobs:

1. Click the Jobs icon at the top of your LinkedIn homepage.
2. Click into the Search bar on the top of the page and search by keywords, title, skill, or a company name.
    o   You can also select from the job roles suggested by LinkedIn based on your qualification and experience. Please make sure that you've updated your LinkedIn profile with your experience, education, and other information.
    o   You'll be directed to the search results page where you'll see a list of job postings that suit your job role and location preference.

3. Use the filters options at the top of the search results page to filter the results. Note: Once you've applied all the filters, you can switch on the Set Alert toggle and set job alerts.
4. Click the job posting to view the job description and apply for the job if the job suits your requirement.

Note: There are two types of job postings on LinkedIn

- Easy Apply: This allows you to apply for the job on LinkedIn.
- Apply: You'll be redirected to the company or third-party website where you can apply for the job externally.

LinkedIn provides endless opportunities for creative job seekers. The following companies you are interested in will keep you up to date on their activities. Finding and following executives in the companies and reading their posts are also great opportunities. I am a huge fan of LinkedIn.

FACEBOOK

Facebook can be a blessing and a curse. It just depends on how you use it. While the platform serves as an amazing social tool to bring people together, it also can be problematic for people in the business world that share a little too much of their personal lives on the platform.

My first recommendation for your Facebook account would be to make it private. That way only the people you invite will have access. Beyond that, my advice is simple, THINK BEFORE YOU POST! If companies conduct a search on LinkedIn, they will usually also glance at your Facebook page as well. Do you really want photos from your last spring break party weighing into their hiring decision? Of course not, so keep your feed clean. Think long and hard about your choices on social media as they can come back to haunt you long after the post is uploaded.

OTHER SOCIAL MEDIA

Regardless of the platform, the most important lesson you can learn about social media when it comes to business hiring is that if it's not something you would be comfortable sharing during an interview, don't post it. Companies, most often, are looking for employees who demonstrate good judgment and comport themselves professionally, so use those characteristics as "sniff tests" before you hit submit. Think, also, about the culture of the workspace you are seeking to enter. For example, if you are seeking a job at an organization that is grounded in a bipartisan or non-political atmosphere, you may wish to avoid posting about contentious political topics, etcetera.

Chapter 12:

Your References

Thinking is the hardest work there is, which is probably the reason, so few engage in it.

Henry Ford

Having available references to provide to a potential employer is an important part of your interview preparation. In today's world, companies will check your social media pages and, in most cases, will call one or more of the references that you provide. For this reason (and also simply as a good life practice), I am a big advocate of staying in touch with the people in your lives.

Securing references may seem especially stressful if you are at the very beginning of your career. Think about a teacher who encouraged you, a coach who trained you, or even a pastor who inspired you. These can all be great references when you are starting out. After you have spent time working, make sure you keep track of supervisors that like you and encourage you.

People that you worked alongside are also great references. Finally, if you serve in a managerial role, make sure you develop long-term relationships with people who worked for you.

When hiring, I would always ask applicants for at least one of each of these three references:

1. Name, address, and phone number of someone who you previously worked for (a boss).
2. Name, address, and phone number of someone who you worked with (a peer).
3. Name, address, and phone number of someone who worked for you (a subordinate, if applicable).

The time to begin working on your list of references is long before you ever need them. This may seem like common sense, but this step is often overlooked during the job search process. Reach out to people who might be willing to provide a reference for you and get their permission *in advance*. It's also important, when you reach out, that you ask your contact whether they are willing to provide a positive reference. It's not a given that all references are positive, so please choose carefully. Having a solid list of references is just one more way of interview preparation that will help build your confidence.

Typically, I do not provide references unless a company asks for them, although occasionally references are required on an initial job application form. Asking for references is one way that a company signals that it is showing strong interest in you as a candidate, which is always a positive sign. Sometimes, hiring managers may request references on the spot or with little-to-no turnaround time, which can be stressful— particularly if you have not prepared in advance. That is why waiting until the company asks for your references before you ask your contacts is a big mistake! By assembling your list in advance, you are not only demonstrating to the company that you are prepared, but you are also avoiding putting any personal relationships in jeopardy.

If the company does ask you for your list of references, make sure you immediately notify everyone on your list that they might get a call or an email so they can be on the lookout for the incoming request. I have received reference check calls from companies for someone who I supported, but who put me on their list without telling me and I accidentally ignored the calls, thinking they were spam. Don't be that person: plan ahead!

The request for references usually occurs when a company is narrowing down the list of candidates to a final few. By this time, you should have a solid handle on what skills and attributes the company is looking for. It is prudent to send your references a simple email notification that looks something like this:

Dear Bruce,

I have been interviewing with XYZ company during the past couple of weeks. As expected, they have asked me for references, and I have given them your contact information. Thank you so much for your willingness to provide a reference for me. If possible, here are a few things I would like you to emphasize about my skillsets.

1. *My leadership skills*
2. *My ability to build high performance teams*
3. *My organizational skills*
4. *My fiscal management skills*

I believe these four areas would be of great interest to the company so anything you can say on my behalf would be greatly appreciated!

Sincerely,

Peter

Some companies or organizations may request written letters of recommendation from your references as part of the job selection process. This can cause the applicant additional stress and underscores the wisdom in having spoken to your references early during your job hunt process. More often than not, especially if your references are people with fairly high seniority in a previous company that you have worked for, they may have a tight schedule and ask you to write a draft of the letter for them to submit. You may feel uncomfortable singing your own praises, but much like the email above, it is your opportunity to demonstrate specific ways in which you have previously demonstrated the skills that the company is looking for. When reaching out to your reference, it may be helpful to include a copy of your resume to refresh them of your experiences.

Organizing your references is a lifelong pursuit. Make sure to stay in contact with those special connections that will sing your praises when needed. In today's world of social media, it is not difficult, but you should always keep a hard copy of your references in your Interview notebook. That way you will always have a place to start when you begin a new search.

Interview story #11

One of the top performers in the company I ran had made a few dumb mistakes during the previous year that had gotten them into trouble with my management. None of the offenses had risen to the level of termination, so I had defended them. After one incident where, again, I believed that the individual had made an honest mistake and I had bailed them out, they abruptly quit going to work for one of my biggest competitors. They provided no notice, and I didn't hear from them after that. Four years passed and I was sitting in my office and received a call from a recruiter. He was looking for a reference for none other than the employee who had disappeared 4 years ago. The recruiter pressed me for information, and I told him that I had not had any contact in four years and could not provide any reference at all. The recruiter asked me again and said, "do you realize that your refusal to provide a reference has to be marked down as a bad reference?" I told him that it was my only option, and he could score it any way he wanted. To my astonishment, about 20 minutes after I hung up with the recruiter, the former employee called me to find out why I would give him a reference, demonstrating that while he had my contact information, he only used it when hadn't received something he needed something from me.

Moral of the Story: Call your references in advance. Make sure they are ready, willing, and able to provide a positive reference for you. If they are the least bit hesitant, move on to someone else.

Closing Thoughts

Our greatest weakness lies in giving up. The most certain
way to succeed is to try just one more time.
– Thomas Edison

The job search can be incredibly challenging. It can be frustrating and at times downright cruel. Rejection is difficult to handle during a job search. You can, and will, experience rejection. A successful search requires perseverance and tenacity. You must stay in the game. Keep working on your stories. Refine them, develop them, practice them, and own them. Your attitude is the most powerful tool in your tool chest. A strong positive attitude, coupled with great preparation and organization, will position you for maximum success in every interview. Now, go make it happen!

Thinking

If you think you are beaten, you are
If you think you dare not, you don't,
If you like to win, but you think you can't
It is almost certain you won't.

If you think you'll lose, you're lost
For out of the world we find,
Success begins with a fellow's will
It's all in the state of mind.

If you think you are outclassed, you are
You've got to think high to rise,
You've got to be sure of yourself before
You can ever win a prize.

Life's battles don't always go
To the stronger or faster man,
But soon or late the one who wins
Is the one WHO THINKS THEY CAN!

- Walter D. Wintle

- ☐ Administration
- ☐ Cooperative
- ☐ Independence
- ☐ Problem solving
- ☐ Analytical
- ☐ Decision Making
- ☐ Judgement
- ☐ Productivity
- ☐ Appearance
- ☐ Delegating
- ☐ Presentations
- ☐ Coachability
- ☐ Fairness
- ☐ Negotiating
- ☐ Social Media
- ☐ Compassion
- ☐ Knowledge

- ☐ Values
- ☐ Dependability
- ☐ Leadership
- ☐ Professionalism
- ☐ Coaching
- ☐ Flexibility
- ☐ Networking
- ☐ Strategic
- ☐ Honesty
- ☐ Performance
- ☐ Competent
- ☐ Patience
- ☐ approachability
- ☐ Versatility
- ☐ Winner
- ☐ Personable
- ☐ Humor

- ☐ Responsible
- ☐ Concentration
- ☐ Integrity
- ☐ Perseverance
- ☐ Action Oriented
- ☐ Conscientious
- ☐ Initiative
- ☐ Persuasiveness
- ☐ Adaptability
- ☐ Creativity
- ☐ Innovation
- ☐ Planning
- ☐ Confidence
- ☐ Follow-up
- ☐ Organization
- ☐ Self Motivated
- ☐ Wisdom

- ☐ Attendance
- ☐ Directing Others
- ☐ Learning Ability
- ☐ Public Speaking
- ☐ Accuracy
- ☐ Drive
- ☐ Listening
- ☐ Resourcefulness
- ☐ Team Building
- ☐ Discretion
- ☐ Loyalty
- ☐ Achievement
- ☐ Conflict Resolution
- ☐ Goal Setting
- ☐ Openness
- ☐ Team Player
- ☐ Competent

- ☐ Budgeting
- ☐ Empathy
- ☐ Management
- ☐ Responsive
- ☐ Career Ambition
- ☐ Enthusiasm
- ☐ Caring
- ☐ Ethics
- ☐ Motivation
- ☐ Service
- ☐ Communications
- ☐ Gracious
- ☐ Operations
- ☐ Thorough
- ☐ Composure
- ☐ Hard Working
- ☐ Maturity

Made in United States
Troutdale, OR
03/07/2024

18283298R00070